The Wreck of tl

The Worst Maritime Disaster on the West Coast

By Brian K. Crawford

The Crawford Press
San Anselmo, California

David Higgins

Early on a gray, dark morning in 1875, David William Higgins, a forty-one-year-old journalist and author, walked down to the docks at Victoria British Columbia, to see off a friend on the steamship *Pacific*, just about to depart for San Francisco.

Higgins was born in Halifax, but raised in New York City. He'd learned the printing trade as a youth. In 1856, he'd come to California to seek his

David Higgins

fortune. But the Mother Lode was played out, and Higgins instead started a newspaper in San Francisco, the *Morning Call*. It was successful, but when news of a new gold strike along the Fraser River in British Columbia arrived the following year, he sold the paper to join the throngs of gold-crazed hopefuls flooding to the north. He dabbled in mining, then opened a store catering to the miners. By 1858, Higgins, like tens of thousands of others, drifted south again. While passing through Victoria, a chance encounter with Amor de Cosmos[1], who owned the newspaper *British*

---

[1] Born William Alexander Smith (1825-1897) in Nova Scotia. In 1845 he converted to Mormonism and went to the California gold rush. In 1854 he petitioned the California Legislature to change his name to Amor de Cosmos (Lover of the Universe). In 1858 he went to the Fraser River gold rush, then started his paper in Victoria. He was active in liberal politics and in 1872 was elected the second Premier of British

Colonist, resulted in a job for Higgins. Soon he had again started his own paper, the *Victoria Daily Chronicle.* In 1863 he bought out his former employer and amalgamated the two papers as the *Daily British Colonist*[2].

On this chilly, windy morning, he was coming down to meet with a man who was about to sail for the States. The ship, a side-wheel steamer named the *S. S. Pacific,* was at the dock, having come down from Puget Sound the day before with a few score passengers from Seattle and Tacoma in the Washington Territory.

Now a jostling crowd swarmed the dock, many of them miners returning from the latest gold strike in Cassiar, in the far north of the Province. Some of these had struck it rich and were carrying sacks of gold dust they were eager to take back to the States. Others had not, and were begging at the ticket windows for cheaper fares home. Fifty or so Chinese miners all seemed to be talking simultaneously among themselves in their strange sing-song language. Weaving through these noisy throngs were small knots of first-class passengers, followed by porters pushing carts piled high with luggage. Animals were everywhere – draft horses pulling drays and heavy wagons, single and double carriages, traps, surreys, and buggies. There was even an equestrian troupe overseeing the loading of their precious animals aboard the ship. The steamer's yards were serving as cargo cranes, swinging nets full of boxes and barrels over the heads of the crowd. Women tried to keep their over-excited children beside them in the press of people. Higgins slowly made his way to the gang plank and finally boarded the ship. Years later, he would describe his visit:

On the morning of the 4th of November, 1875,
having business with a gentleman named Conway,

Columbia. He became more and more eccentric, was declared insane, and died in Victoria in 1897, aged 71.

[2] Which survives today as the *Victoria Times-Colonist.*

one of the *Pacific's* passengers, I was on the wharf before the hour which the steamer was advertised to sail – nine A. M. I found the boat so crowded that the crew could scarcely move about the decks in discharge of their duties. The morning was dark and lowering. Heavy clouds moved slowly overhead. A fall of rain had preceded the coming of the sun, but there were no signs that indicated worse weather than is usual in this latitude in the fall of the year. I think I must have known at least one hundred of the persons who took passage that day. Captain and Mrs. Otis Parsons and child, with Mrs. Thorne, a sister of Mrs. Parsons, were amongst those to whom I said farewell and wished bon voyage. The Captain had just sold his interest in the Fraser river steamers for a sum exceeding $40,000.00 in gold, and he was taking his family to San Francisco to enjoy their new wealth. Mrs. Parsons had been on the stage. She came to San Francisco in 1856 as the contralto in a group known as The Pennsylvanians. She had a voice of great sweetness and power and was a decided favorite with all lovers of good music. Parsons was attracted to her by her fine acting and singing, and married her while she was a member of the Fanny Morgan Phelps Company, which held the boards at the Victoria Theatre for a long time.

Having said goodbye to Parsons and his family, I reached with difficulty a place where Miss Fannie Palmer, youngest daughter of Professor Digby Palmer, stood. This young lady was a bright and lovely member of Victoria society. She was most popular, and naturally attracted a large circle of admirers. By a number of these she was besieged when I advanced to say farewell. Her fond mother was in the group that surrounded the fair girl, whose

3

sweet face was more than usually animated in anticipation of the round of pleasure that awaited her upon arrival in San Francisco.

Every class, every nationality, every age were assembled on the deck of that vessel. The last hands I grasped were those of S. P. Moody, of the Moodyville Sawmill Co., and Frank Garesche, private banker and Wells, Fargo & Co.'s agent. As I descended the gangplank I met a lady with a little boy in her arms. The way was steep and I volunteered to carry the little fellow aboard. He was handed to me, and I toiled up the plank and delivered him to his mother when she, too, had gained the deck. The wee, blue-eyed boy put up his lips to be kissed, and waved his little hands as I turned to go, and then mother and child were swallowed up in the dense throng, and I saw them no more.

The ship, as I have said, was billed to sail at nine o'clock. It was nearly ten o'clock when Captain Howell appeared on the bridge and the order was given to cast off. As the vessel swung off, the multitude on the wharf gave three rousing cheers to speed departing friends on their way. The response was loud and hearty, and hands and handkerchiefs were waved and last messages exchanged until the vessel had disappeared around the first point.

A belated Englishman, who had passed the previous night in a wild revel, and who had taken a ticket by the *Pacific* was the "last man" on this occasion. As the vessel passed out of the harbor, the belated one appeared on the wharf with his hand bag and a steamer trunk. He shouted and signaled, but all to no purpose. The boat kept on her way, and the man danced up and down in his rage. Then he sat down on his trunk and cursed the boat and all

4

its belongings. His profanity was awful to hear and quite original. As it appeared to do him good, no one interrupted him. When I left, he was still cursing.

On the corner of Government and Fort Streets, as I passed along a few minutes later, I saw Mrs. Digby Palmer standing. She was gazing with glistening eyes towards the outer harbor. Where the Rithet Wharf now stands there was on the shore quite a grove of tall forest trees. Above the tops of these trees the smoke of the departing steamer was rising in great black billows and losing itself in space. It was this smoke Mrs. Palmer was watching. As I approached, she exclaimed, "I'm seeing the last of Fannie!"

The *S.S. Pacific*

The steamship *Pacific* was built in New York City by William H. Brown, and was launched September 24, 1850. She was a wooden side-wheel steamer of 1,003 tons, 225 feet long, with two decks and three masts. She was driven by a single vertical-beam steam engine built by the Archimedes Iron Works of New York and was licensed to carry 203 passengers.

She was initially operated by the United States Mail Steamship Company on the run between New Orleans and Chagres, Panama, carrying some of the flood of prospectors trying to get to the California gold fields. But while there were many steamers running from the U. S. to Panama, there were few on the Pacific side to take them to California. So on March 19, 1851, the *Pacific* sailed from New York around Cape Horn to San Francisco, arriving July 2, a passage of 106 days. She was then sold to Cornelius Vanderbilt, who put her on the run between Panama and San

Francisco. She delivered thousands of miners to California. But at the end of the gold rush she was laid up as no longer fit for service. Along with hundreds of other ships abandoned by their crews, she moldered on the mudflats of San Francisco Bay for several years.

In 1858, gold was discovered on the Fraser River in British Columbia, and soon men were again clamoring for transportation. The old *Pacific* was bought by the Merchants Accommodation Line, repaired, and put into service between San Francisco and the Columbia River.

On July 18, 1861, she struck Coffin Rock in the Columbia River and sank. She was raised and repaired and again put back into service. In 1863 she was purchased by the Oregon and San Diego Steamship Line. The next year she was sold to Holladay and Brenham, and then in 1872 to the Pacific Mail Steamship Line. Demand for transport waned, and the tired old steamer was again left to rot.

Then in 1875, another gold strike, this time at Cassiar, in the far north of British Columbia, started the mad rush for transport all over again. Three partners in San Francisco – Charles Goodall, Christopher Nelson, and George Perkins – purchased the *Pacific* and another superannuated steamer, the *S.S. California,* from Pacific Mail and formed their own steamship company, Goodall and Nelson. They had the ships overhauled and repaired. Both ships were inspected and certified safe by the official Inspector of Hulls in San Francisco, Captain Robert Waterman, though her cargo capacity was reduced from 1,003 to 876 tons.

In spite of this certification, the *Pacific* was now twenty-five years old in an era when steamboats were typically retired after ten or fifteen years. Unlike more modern vessels that were planked on both the outside and inside of their frames, the Pacific was "single-hulled." This made her notoriously leaky, so that cargo had to be stored on the 'tween decks to keep it dry. Such stowage also raised her center of gravity, making her "crank," or subject to rolling.

7

The Passage

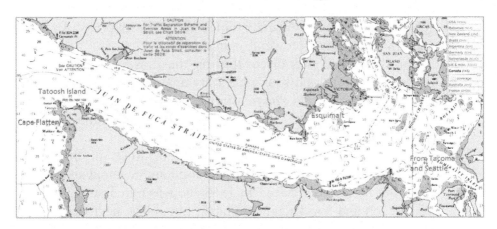

The *S.S. Pacific* was bound from the Strait of Juan de Fuca, separating the United States and Canada, to San Francisco, a passage of about 1,250 miles. She sailed from Seattle to Tacoma, in Puget Sound in the Washington Territory, picking up passengers at both ports. The next day she steamed seventy miles northwest to Esquimalt harbor, the port for the city of Victoria, at the southeastern corner of Vancouver Island. There she took on the majority of her passengers and freight.

From Esquimalt she would steam another seventy miles west and north through the Strait of Fuca toward the open Pacific. The Strait there is from ten to twelves miles wide, with Washington on the left shore and Vancouver Island on the right. The far northwestern tip of Washington is a

Cape Flattery Light on Tatoosh Island

steep headland named Cape Flattery, with a group of small

rocky islets collectively called Tatoosh Island just offshore, marked by Cape Flattery Lighthouse. After rounding Tatoosh Island, she would turn south and continue along the coasts of the Washington and Oregon Territories, then the final 250 miles of northern California to the Golden Gate.

The entire coast is steep and rocky and there are very few ports. At that time there were few lighthouses to mark headlands and harbor entrances, though they did exist in California at Point Arena, Point Reyes, and Point Bonita at the entrance to San Francisco.

In November, when the *Pacific* sailed, there are frequent storms and gales, often accompanied by fog, along the whole stretch of coast. A cold current, the Humboldt Current, flows down from Alaska, speeding southbound vessels, but also pushing them toward the rocky shore. Dozens of vessels large and small had already been lost on the same passage.

The Passengers

Captain Otis Parsons stood at the rail, watching his friend Higgins making his way back to the dock. He saw him pass a child up the gangway and smiled when the toddler reached up and kissed him. Though Parsons had spent years as a captain of steamships, on this trip he was just a passenger.

There was a cold breeze coming in off the Strait of Juan de Fuca, and Parsons pulled close his wife Jennie. Their eighteen-month-old son

Captain Otis Parsons

was in her arms, pressed between them, snuggled into the warmth of their fur coats. After years of struggle as a seaman, gold miner, storekeeper, ferry operator, and steamer captain, Otis had finally made his fortune running a line of steamships where no one thought a steamer could go – delivering eager miners up the Fraser River to the Cassiar gold fields. Every winter when the river became impassable, the Parsons sailed to San Francisco to enjoy the social season in that fashionable city. But this would be their last trip.

The steamer business on the frontier was full of risk – unpredictable weather, boiler explosions, and groundings. Several of his steamers had been lost. Now, as the latest gold rush subsided, they had decided to retire permanently to San Francisco. He had sold the whole outfit – a fleet of steamers, ticket offices, agents, warehouses and all, for a very good price. In a strongbox in the ship's safe was $40,000 in gold consigned to him, the proceeds of decades of hard work. Now, with his fortune made, a beautiful and talented wife, and an heir, he was a contented man. He and Jennie were looking forward to their new lives in San Francisco.

Had they known of Captain Parson's history, his fellow passengers might have felt cause for concern, for he had shown a remarkable propensity for finding himself shipwrecked on this same stretch of coastline. In 1866 he had taken passage from San Francisco to Victoria on the Hudson's Bay Company steamer *LaBouchere*. Their first night out they struck Point Reyes in a fog and foundered with the loss of two men. The remaining one hundred-thirty passengers and crew reached shore and hiked to San Rafael. Four years later, Parsons was a passenger on the North Pacific Transportation Company steamer *Active* when she struck a rock in the fog at Spanish Flat, twenty-five miles north of Mendocino, on June 5, 1870. She was run ashore and the passengers, luggage, and mail saved. And just the year before, he had been aboard the steamer *Prince Alfred* when she ran aground on the Potato Patch, just north of the Golden Gate, on June 14, 1874. All passengers and crew were saved, but in all three cases the vessels had been a total loss. So Parsons could be seen as either remarkably lucky or remarkably unlucky. He was certainly familiar with the dangers of the sea and this passage in particular.

As he watched the preparations for departure, he didn't like what he saw. With years of experience in command of similar ships, he knew that the *Pacific* was designed to carry no more than 250 passengers and crew. And even that number was a lot of weight for a ship a quarter-century old. The new partnership Goodall and Nelson that owned her was in direct competition with the long-established Pacific Mail, which owned nearly every other passenger ship on the coast. To entice customers, Goodall sometimes cut the normal ten dollar fare to five dollars, barely enough to make a profit.

11

Groups of four or more went for half-fare, and children were free. As they were boarding, Parsons had noticed agents selling cut-rate tickets and even handing out free passes to the desperate miners, just to take customers away from Pacific Mail.

But one man who rushed up with his wife and child at the last minute found the prices raised. Samuel Styles had inquired the day before and been told the fare was ten dollars, but now that the ship was about to leave and cabins were at a premium, the ticket agent demanded fifteen. Styles paid the money and bought a ticket for his wife and child, then saw them aboard.

Parsons started feeling more uneasy as he watched yet more miners pressing forward to the gangplank, and the ship's officers waving more aboard. He could see more than two hundred people on the deck already, and could hear more on the hurricane deck above him. Assuming most cabin passengers were below, stowing their luggage and settling in, he estimated there must be at least four hundred people aboard[3]. The passage promised to be crowded and uncomfortable at best – and perhaps rowdy. All those miners would be noisily gambling the whole passage, trying to redistribute the wealth of the lucky ones. Well, Parsons had already telegraphed to book rooms in the Cosmopolitan, their favorite hotel in San Francisco, for Friday night. By tomorrow night they would be warm and safely ensconced in its luxurious rooms.

---

[3] David Higgins guessed five hundred.

12

Captain Parson's wife snuggled against her family. Jennie Parsons was thirty-four, and still a beautiful woman. She was excited to be returning to San Francisco. She had been there many times and was well known there as an actress and singer. She had retained her maiden name of Jennie Mandeville as her stage name, and most people still knew her by that name rather than the more recent Mrs. Parsons.

Jennie Mandeville Parsons

She and her younger sisters Agatha and Alicia had been performing as the Mandeville Sisters ever since they arrived from Ireland as teenagers. They had first come to San Francisco nearly twenty years before, filling the American Theatre and Maguire's Opera House to standing room only. She still remembered their glowing review that said, "The girls possessed great beauty and grace of figure, and were endowed with sweet voices and dramatic ability." Their brother Cal had joined the company as an actor, promoter, singer, and songwriter. Many of his songs were well-known and published as sheet music across the country.

The trio was disbanded in 1858, when Agatha left for Italy to complete her musical education. The talented young singer studied under the foremost masters, and finally made her debut in grand opera. She sang in all the major cities of the Old World, and received the highest reviews. She then returned to America and appeared in leading operatic roles, adding new laurels to her fame by her sweet singing. Agatha had married a physician, William Noyes States, and had two children, William and Beatrice States. Sadly, she had died of consumption in 1874, aged just thirty-two.

The remaining siblings Jennie, Alicia, and Cal toured the country with the Bates Troupe of actors and entertainers. They formed a singing group called the Pennsylvanians, although none were from that state. Alicia married Charles Thorne Jr., a son of a famous actor, and himself possessed of great ability. Jennie remained single till later in life, when she married Wadsworth Porter, a livery-stable keeper of San Francisco. He went mad over losses at the gaming table and died in the state hospital in Stockton.

Jennie joined the Fanny Morgan Phelps Company and toured the Northwest doing serious drama on a raw frontier (they performed the first-ever Shakespeare play in Seattle: "Taming of the Shrew" in 1875). While on tour in Victoria, having been six years a widow, she married the sea captain Otis Parsons in 1871. After years of loneliness, she was finally settled and happy and a new mother.

The Parsons had been booked to leave on the steamship *Dakota* on October 30th. But then news arrived to change their plans. Jennie's brother Cal had gotten himself in trouble up in Fort Wrangel, Alaska. In September he and two partners were caught selling whiskey to Indians and went to jail. The government now agreed to let them go if they left the country. Cal was scheduled to leave from Victoria on the *Pacific* on the 4th, and his wife Bella and their son would join him there. Their sister Alicia Mandeville Thorne decided to accompany them – the Mandeville family was leaving Canada for good. So Otis and Jenny delayed their departure by five days so they could all travel together. Cal and his cronies were released into the custody of a marshal and sent to Vancouver on the steamer *California*. So there were seven in their party – Otis and Jennie Parsons and their son, Cal and Bella Mandeville and their son, and Alicia Thorne. The passage promised to be an enjoyable family reunion, but one wonders what they said to Cal after he arrived at the dock in irons and was unshackled in full view of the other passengers.

The departure time of nine o'clock passed and there was no lessening of activity on the deck and wharf. Cargo and luggage was still being hoisted aboard, and yet more people were crowding up the gangplank. Chatting with some of the other first-class passengers, the Parson-Mandeville party soon encountered friends they knew from show business, who had come with the ship from Seattle.

Malcolm Douglas Hurlburt was from the small town of Greene, in upstate New York. He had grown up around horses and became an expert trainer and breeder. Two of his neighbors, Leroy and James Cowles, also trained horses. They had trained a pair of horses so they could be driven, stopped, and backed up without the use of reins, and started giving exhibitions.

Malcom Douglas Hurlburt

They toured the country and trained horses for Barnum and Bailey's Circus. Malcolm Hurlburt and a friend, Andrew H. Rockwell, had been training three horses they thought had exceptional intelligence and ability, named Tiger, Star, and Mazeppa. They talked to the Cowles brothers and formed a partnership, The Rockwell and Hurlburt Equestrienne Troupe, in which the Cowles helped train Hurlburt's horses. Soon they could drive a three-horse carriage without bridle or reins. The troupe gave exhibitions and taught classes in horse training. They had two greyhounds and five other horses, all trained to do tricks, but the star of their shows was the huge beautiful white gelding Mazeppa. He was named for the poem by Lord Byron about Ivan Mazeppa, a Ukrainian Cossack who was punished by being tied naked to a stallion and sent racing across the countryside (he survived, a sort of Lord Godiva). Wondering audiences said the magnificent horse was so intelligent he could do everything but talk.

The show was very successful and the partners did well. By 1875, Hurlburt had bought another farm in the town of Greene and had seven children. Andrew Rockwell married Hurlburt's sister Elles, and he and Hurlburt wrote a book titled *The Education of the Horse*. The partners Malcolm Hurlburt, James Cowles, and Andrew Rockwell, with Andrew's wife Elles Hurlburt Rockwell and their advance agent James Douglas Crowley, had been on tour for about a year when the six of them, six horses, and two dogs, with all their equipment and carriages, boarded the *Pacific*. Two nights before their departure, they had given an exhibition in the streets of Seattle that was very widely attended. On the day of their departure, too late for them to have seen it, the *Puget Sound Dispatch* published a review:

> Horse Training. —Rockway [sic] & Hurlburt, the celebrated horse trainers, gave their first public exhibition at noon to-day. They drove horses around the streets without reins, guiding them with whips with the greatest possible ease. They afterwards invited the crowd inside their large tent, where they gave an exhibition of their wonderful trained horse Mazeppa, putting him through some truly remarkable feats. Messrs. Rockwell & Hurlburt finish today their lessons in horse-training. They have had a small class and instructed

16

them thoroughly in their plan of breaking and training horses without cruelty.

So there were two groups of professional entertainers aboard the *Pacific*, and possibly many more. It was November, and many performers preferred to avoid a Canadian winter. There were no trains between California and the territories at that time, so any companies touring the West Coast had to travel by the coastal steamers. One old-time showman, writing anonymously many years later as "The Old 'Un", said that he had had forty-three show business friends aboard the *Pacific* that day.

The other two friends to whom David Higgins said goodbye that morning were men who had become wealthy from the Canadian gold rush. Sewell Prescott Moody, usually called "Sue", was born in Maine in 1834. In 1849, as a boy of fourteen, he crossed the country to San Francisco with his family in a covered wagon. He went to British Columbia in 1861 in the Cariboo gold

S. P. Moody

rush, and like many before him, found that it was easier to make money selling supplies to miners than by digging for gold. His family had been in the lumber business in Maine, so he formed a partnership and cut a big load of lumber to ship up the Fraser River to the mines, where lumber was in great demand. Unfortunately, the steamer (perhaps one of

Captain Parson's) ran aground and could not be shifted for six weeks, while other lumber steamers passed it by. Moody then bought some land at Burrard's Inlet, near Victoria, and established a second sawmill. This one was very successful, and within a few years he was sending shipments to California, Hawaii, Peru, China, Australia, New Zealand, and Great Britain. In 1869 he married Janet Watson and they had two children.

A company town grew up around the mill, still called Moodyville. The original plant was powered by water, but later converted to steam. In 1873 the plant burned down and was rebuilt, this time powered by the engines of *HMS Sparrowhawk*, a gunboat retired by the Royal Navy.

Moody kept a tight rein on Moodyville. It was purely a company town, ruled by Sue Moody. He refused to allow liquor sales, but he built a school, church, library, and a Masonic lodge. He also paid for a telegraph line from Victoria.

Jean Garesche was a nobleman who fled the terror of the French Revolution and landed in Santo Domingo in the West Indies. He later moved to Delaware, where his son Francis John Garesche was born in 1830. By 1850, Francis was in Calaveras County with the Gold Rush. Five years later, he married Clara Mallet in San Francisco. They had eight sons and three daughters, though four of them died young – three in 1866 alone. He became the agent for Wells Fargo & Co. in Victoria. His knowledge of both mining and finance served him well. For nearly two decades there had been a series of gold rushes that flared and faded in British Columbia – the Queen Charlottes Rush and the Cariboo and the Fraser River and half a dozen others. As each field was claimed out or went bust, thousands of hard, desperate men swarmed from one to the next – a cycle of immense labor, immense suffering, and, very occasionally, immense wealth. Frank Garesche and Sue Moody became partners in the

Eureka mine, one of the richest silver discoveries in the area, and made a fortune. Frank built a large commercial block in Victoria that still bears his name. He partnered with Alexander Green, who had made his fortune in another gold rush in Australia, and they formed the Garesche & Green Bank. Green built one of the most expensive and elaborate mansions in Victoria[4]. Frank Garesche sold his portion of the Eureka mine and had almost $30,000 in gold with him on this trip. He planned to join his wife Clara and their son Herman on a tour to England. As the agent of Wells Fargo, he was also the official escort for $79,000 in gold being shipped to San Francisco by that company.

Another man who had done well in Canada was aboard. Joseph Hellmuth, born in Germany around 1823, came to California in 1850 during the Gold Rush. He married a French woman, Odile Farg-Aly, and set up a vegetable business in Marysville. He later moved to Portland, Oregon Territory, and then Walla Walla, in the Washington Territory. Having "acquired a handsome competency," he and his wife were on the first leg of a return trip to Europe.

There were at least two successful miners who could afford first class cabins – Dennis Kane and Richard Lyon. They were the prospectors who first found gold in the Cassiar and sparked the rush. They were returning as wealthy men. It is very likely that they too were carrying large amounts of gold.

Other notables aboard included Henry C. Victor, a naval engineer and husband of the then well-known author Francis Fuller Victor[5]; Hon. George T. Vining, who had served in the Oregon Legislature and was then a candidate for

---

[4] Now the Spencer Mansion and Art Gallery of Greater Victoria.
[5] Later to become the foremost historian of the Oregon Territory

Secretary of State, accompanying a shipment of his hops to San Francisco; and Fred D. Hard, former Special Postal Agent for Washington Territory.

Elizabeth Moote, 25, was the daughter of former Victoria mayor and newspaper editor James McMillan. She was returning to her husband Samuel David Moote in San Francisco following a family christening.

The Crew

The man responsible for all these people was Captain Jefferson Davis Howell, master of the *S.S. Pacific*. He was born in Natchez, Mississippi, in 1841, the last of eleven children. His father William Burr Howell, a decorated naval officer in the war of 1812, named him for his friend Jefferson Davis, who had married William's daughter Varina Banks Howell.

Captain J. D. Howell

Jeff was educated at Annapolis, but when the Civil War erupted, he enlisted in the Confederate army. Two years later he joined the Confederate Navy as midshipman and served at Charleston, in the James River Squadron, and afterwards at Charleston in charge of a picket boat. After the fall of Charleston, he became a Lieutenant of Artillery in the Naval brigade under General Rafael Semmes, who a week before had been Admiral Semmes of the Confederate Navy. He surrendered under General Lee's cartel and joined his sister Mrs. Jefferson Davis and her family at Washington, Georgia, where the presidential staff fled after the fall of Richmond. He was with the president at the time of his capture and they were both imprisoned at Fort Monroe at Hampton Roads. When he was released, he went to Savannah, Georgia, but was again imprisoned. Then he

21

joined his brother in Canada and accompanied him to England. Returning by way of Portland, Maine, he was again arrested and sent to Fort Warren, where he was detained for a few weeks and released. He complained to the government about his treatment, claiming he had done no more than his duty as an officer, he had never been charged with any crimes, and at his surrender he and all the rebels were promised amnesty. He asked to be permitted to volunteer with the Canadian forces, but his request was refused. In desperation, he went to New York and took a berth as an able seaman. When he returned from his voyages, he worked for a time at the *New York News*, but he grew tired of newspaper work and went back to his first love, the sea. He sailed as quartermaster on a ship bound for China, and from there went to San Francisco about 1870 and entered the service of the Pacific Mail Steamship Company. He served as mate on three successive steamers, then was promoted to Captain and commanded six other vessels before the *Pacific*. Though only thirty-four, he had many years of experience at sea, much of that in command. If anyone knew the strengths and weaknesses of his ship, it was he.

The *Pacific* was licensed to carry 203 passengers – 115 in first class and 88 in second, and had a crew of 52. Neither Captain Howell nor anyone else knew just how many people were aboard that day. Thirty-five had come with them from Tacoma and the agent in Victoria sold another 132 tickets. The purser had sold at least 20 tickets at the gangplank and dozens more had scrambled aboard at the last minute, none of whose names had been recorded. No one even bothered to count the children because they traveled free.

There were supposed to be eight lifeboats, but she carried only five – two large boats, the launch and the longboat, each capable of carrying fifty, forward of the paddle boxes, and three smaller boats aft, each carrying fifteen – a maximum of 145.

If Captain Howell was concerned about the overcrowding, it is not recorded. After all, the *Pacific* had once carried seven hundred miners to Victoria when the Fraser River gold rush was in its heady opening days. Of course, that was almost twenty years before when she was relatively new, and before she had been left to rot on the mudflats of San Francisco Bay.

It was nearly ten o'clock before the last passengers and cargo were aboard. In the hold were 2,000 sacks of oats, 300 bales of hops shipped by George Vining of Puyallup, a large quantity of potatoes. 261 animal hides, 11 casks of furs, 31 barrels of cranberries, 10 cords of wood bolts, 280 tons of coal, 18 tons of general merchandise, 10 tons of sundries, six horses, two buggies, two cases of opium and a strongbox containing $79,200 in cash. Captain Howell had directed that the hops and oats be stored on the 'tween decks because the leaky old ship frequently had several feet of water sloshing in the bilge.

Finally the cargo and gear was secured and the ship was ready. At a few minutes to ten, Captain Howell directed his first officer, A. N. McDonaugh, to get under way. McDonaugh was an experienced officer, having commanded several steamships between San Francisco and Yuma for the Colorado River Steamship Company. In February, he was sued for libel by one of his passengers. He was found not guilty, but perhaps the notoriety caused him to be demoted to first mate. Like Captain Parsons, he had been shipwrecked on this same coast before. In July, he had been first mate on the steamer *Eastport* when she went aground on Point Arena. While getting the passengers into a lifeboat, one of the falls broke and dumped the passengers into the sea. A woman and her two children were drowned. This could not have reflected favorably on the first officer.

Dock lines were singled up. The second officer, Mr. A. Wells, used the engine room telegraph to call for slow ahead, and the steamer slowly pulled away from the dock.

Passengers lined the starboard rail, exchanging shouted greetings to their friends on the dock, causing the ship to list to starboard. Meanwhile, the purser had men hastily building temporary bunks to try to get sleeping room for the scores of miners who had come aboard at the last minute. Steerage passengers would have to find places to sleep in sheltered corners.

As the steamer turned slowly out of the harbor into the Strait of Juan de Fuca, Captain Howell noted that the starboard list he had noticed at the dock had not corrected itself as the passengers moved away from the rail. The crew of a dredger working in the bay also noticed the marked list as the *Pacific* steamed past. The cargo may have been stowed unevenly in the rush to get away, or perhaps the sheer number of people aboard made the ship top-heavy. Captain Howell directed Mr. McDonaugh to see if he could bring the ship to an even keel.

The first officer's solution was to set a group of seamen to pumping seawater into the boats on the port side. The ship gradually straightened up, but then rolled over to a port list. Officers asked some of the passengers to move over to the starboard side, but the old steamer would not hold a steady attitude even in the calm waters of the Strait. If a storm came up, she would be dangerously crank, or liable to rolling. Captain Howell hoped for a smooth passage.

The *Pacific* turned west toward the open sea, the southwesterly breeze sending the smoke streaming back from her stack – the same plume of smoke being watched at that moment by the unhappy Mrs. Palmer as she stood watching with David Higgins from Victoria.

The steamer rounded Rocky Point on the right, or Vancouver shore, giving it plenty of room to avoid Race Rocks that extend two miles off shore. Then she turned west to run out through the Strait. It would be several hours before they would see Cape Flattery on their left hand. Not until they were well clear of Tatoosh Island, just off the Cape, could they turn south for San Francisco.

At noon the ship's officers changed the watch. First officer McDonaugh turned the bridge over to the second, Mr. Wells, and repeated to him the captain's instructions for the course: west-by-northwest, speed ten knots. A new quartermaster came to the wheel, twenty-year-old Neil O. Henley. Henley was a Scot, born in the Hebrides in 1855, and learned the trade of building ships. He sailed to the East Indies as a teenager, and arrived in San Francisco in August 1875 on the American steamship *Canada*. He had found a berth on the *S. S. Pacific* only a couple of months before. With his shipwright skills, he had spent the morning with Mr. Errickson, the ship's carpenter, building twenty temporary berths in the saloon for passengers without cabins. Now as he took the helm, he studied the sea ahead. The breeze was moderate, but the seas were increasing as they got closer to the open Pacific. Three hours later a lookout reported Cape Flattery on their port bow, and Henley was ordered to come up a few spokes to head closer to the southern side of the Strait.

At four o'clock they approached the cluster of high flat-topped rocks that make up Tatoosh Island, marked by the house and 65-foot tower of Cape Flattery Lighthouse. The light, only Washington's third, was built in 1854, and stood 165 feet above the sea. It was a crucial landfall for arriving mariners trying to find the entrance to the Strait. It was visible twenty miles at sea if the night was clear.

Mr. Wells directed Henley to come around to port to round the island, but warned him that a series of shoals called Duncan's Rocks extended a half-mile from the lighthouse. When Wells was satisfied with Henley's course, he went below to notify the Captain that they had left the Strait and were in the open sea.

Captain Howell could not have been unaware of the fact. The turn had brought the ship's head into the wind, and the swell that was building up started thumping against the bows and throwing spray over the foredeck. The steamer's uncomfortable, irregular rolling increased. But he and the off-duty officers were busy finding sleeping spaces for the hundreds of passengers without cabins, assisted by his off-watch officers: third mate Justus M. Lewis; purser O. Hyte; freight clerk T. H. Bigley; and the night watchman Henry A. Norris.

Those passengers already settled had come in out of the wind into the saloons and dining room, looking for snacks and drinks. The food staff[6] was already busy preparing food. Waiters were moving through the crowded rooms and passageways with heaping platters and trays of drinks.

Down below, in the steam and noise of the boiler room, Chief Engineer Henry Frank Houston, an experienced officer, was in charge. Born in Westphalia Germany in 1833, he had been a steamer engineer on the Hudson River, then since 1853 on the West Coast. He had been Chief Engineer on many different ships. Now at forty-two, he was one of the most experienced engineers on the coast. He was helped by First Assistant

Henry Houston

Engineer D. M. Bassett and Second Assistant Engineer Arthur Jasper Coghlan. They oversaw the "black gang," so

---

[6] First cook J. M. Holdsworth; Second Cook S. Miles; Third Cook C. H. Whiting; the baker, John Molloy; three pantry men, Richard Bell, C. B. Herbert, and Daniel Monroe, the porter Robert Menaimo; stewards H. Jackson, John Martin, and S. McNicols; stewardesses, Hannah Muir and Sarah Minow; and waiters Charles Eisenor, Oscar Clare, John Hardie, James Johnson, James McGinnis, Luke McMerim, J. C. Meza, Andrew Walters, and Alfred York

named because they were usually covered with coal dust[7]. Serving as lookouts, helmsmen, cargo handlers, messengers, mechanics, painters, and any other duty as assigned were the seamen[8].

The crew numbered fifty-two, about average for a ship of this size, though some of the hands were new and had little experience. Certainly, few had practiced a life boat drill.

As the ship punched into the seas on a southerly heading, Quartermaster Henley found some difficulty steering. The ship was top-heavy and kept lurching from side to side with a heavy sluggish feel to the wheel. The sun went down at a quarter till six, and the overcast sky faded to a dark night. Mr. Adams directed one of the men to trim, fill, and light the ship's running lights: red to port, green to starboard, and a white lantern run up to the fore masthead.

At eight o'clock, the watch was relieved by the first mate's watch. Normally a steamer would have six men on deck at all times – the officer of the deck, a quartermaster at the helm, three lookouts, and a seaman to serve as a messenger and steward.

Mr. McDonaugh sent a quartermaster to the helm and assigned a seaman to stand lookout on the bridge. But then, against regulations, he told the rest of the watch to go below and get some sleep. He posted no forward or aft lookout. If a message needed to be sent, only the lookout could do it, leaving no one on deck. McDonaugh then announced that he too was going to bed and turned the watch over to the relatively inexperienced third mate Justus Lewis, though it was not his watch. Henley gratefully turned the wheel over

---

[7] Firemen James Lestrange, Richard Manders, and James O'Neil; coal-passers William Clancey, Frank Palmer, Charles Norris, and Richard Powers; and oilers Frank Elwell, Thomas Lestrange, and R. Errickson, who doubled as the carpenter.

[8] Neil Henley, John Daley, W. Fairfield, Lawrence Guinn, Peter Jamieson, Thomas Kerby, Patrick Moore, John Sherry, and William Wilson.

to his relief helmsman and went below to his berth, which left only three men on watch, none with much experience.

The Orpheus

The clipper ship Orpheus in 1861

Fifty miles south of the *Pacific*, a sailing ship was running north, the southerly wind speeding her along at twelve knots. She was the medium clipper *Orpheus*, 1057 tons, two hundred feet long, built in 1856 for the firm of William F. Weld & Co. of Boston. William Fletcher Weld and his partner Richard Baker, Jr. owned the Weld fleet of clipper ships, one of the largest in the world at that time. Their ships, marked by jet-black hulls and flying the house flag of a racing black horse, were on every sea. The company did not go in for the extreme clippers then favored by designer Donald McKay, with their sharp bows, massive clouds of sail, and incredible speed. Weld favored the medium clipper design – not as fast, admittedly, but safer, requiring fewer hands, and with more cargo carrying capacity. The *Orpheus* made her maiden voyage to California in 180 days, a very poor run for the period. But she made ten other voyages between Boston and California, her best run of 112 days coming in 1868. In the early 1870's she was sold to the C. L. Taylor Company of San Francisco, who employed her in the coal and lumber trade. On this night she was returning from San Francisco in ballast to pick up a cargo of coal in Nanaimo on Vancouver Island.

Her master was Captain Charles A. Sawyer III, 36, from Gloucester, Massachusetts, descended from a long line of mariners. In spite of his youth, he had been at sea nearly twenty years and commanded several ships. He was known as a hard captain and was not liked by his men. On several occasions he had

Captain Charles Sawyer

trouble with his crews and had dealt harshly with them. He referred to his own men as "scoundrels" and was so remote a shipmaster that he was not sure of his own Second Mate's name (James G. Allen, former First Officer of the *Pacific*). In 1869, aged thirty, he married nineteen-year-old Lillie Haskell and six months later they had a daughter Isabella, usually called Mabel. Both Lillie and Mabel were with him

30

on this voyage; Mabel had just turned six. Besides the three officers, the *Orpheus* carried a carpenter, a steward, a boy, and fourteen men before the mast. The steward also had his wife aboard.

For all his experience, Captain Sawyer had not been long on the West Coast and this was only his second passage on this run. He had left San Francisco on October 28th, so he was now seven days out, an average of less than one hundred miles a day. With both wind and current normally from the north, the run to Vancouver was often slow and frustrating. But with the wind behind them, they were finally making better progress. Perhaps for that reason, he had all sail set and was driving the ship as fast as she would go.

After so many days of beating around looking for a favorable wind, Sawyer was not sure of his position, but he believed they were about twenty miles off shore and approaching Cape Flattery. The wind was fresh from the southeast, and his course roughly northwest, running free. He had ordered his crew to keep a sharp eye out for the lighthouse. He had no wish to run onto Tatoosh Island in the darkness, and told his first officer to steer well to port of the light when it was spotted.

At around a quarter to ten that night, the helmsman Charles Thompson reported a single white light on the port bow. The light would disappear for a few minutes, then wink on again. As he studied the faint light, Sawyer noticed that it appeared now directly ahead. The bridge crew couldn't decide if the light was Cape Flattery or the light of a ship. If it was a ship, there should be colored lights to indicate her direction, but none were visible. Could it be Cape Flattery that far west? Nervous now that he might be closer to the shore than he had reckoned, he ordered the helmsman to turn to the left, giving more sea room to the dangerous cape.

The light grew closer and they finally made out both the red and green sidelights. It was a steamer coming toward

31

them from the north. Sawyer kept turning to port toward the light until he had turned right across the wind and the sails thundered back against the masts and the ship stopped. Suddenly the bow of the steamer loomed out of the dark. It blew one blast of its whistle, but in less than thirty seconds its starboard bow had struck his ship a glancing blow just behind the starboard fore chains, smashing in the rail and breaking his planking down to near the copper at the waterline. The steamship ground aft down the clipper's starboard side, carrying away all his starboard braces and rigging on that side. His fore topmast and topgallant masts toppled and went overboard with their masses of yards, sails, and rigging. Someone shouted that the ship was filling with water.

Captain Sawyer bellowed out to the steamer as she surged past, asking them to heave to and send a boat, as he supposed his ship to be sinking; but no one answered his hail, nor did he see any one on her deck. His wife Lillie was so furious at the steamer's indifference that she stormed out on deck shouting angrily and would have clambered aboard the steamer if she had not been restrained. The steamer drifted or steamed away, he was not certain which.

Fearing the worst, the men opened the fore hold and the carpenter went down to investigate. In a few minutes he returned and reported that the damage was above the waterline and the hold was dry. They were not sinking, but they were seriously damaged and partly dismasted. The crew started cutting away the tangle of wreckage and splicing broken lines.

The steamer circled around behind them and came to a stop a mile or two off their port beam. Someone on the steamer called out "Ship ahoy!" three times, very distinctly. The lookouts reported the hail to the captain, but Sawyer just turned away. He was of course concerned about the safety of his own ship – but perhaps he also realized that he had been at fault in approaching the steamer. Perhaps he hoped his ship would not be identified by the steamer. Soon afterward he saw a light flash which he took for a signal that they had heard his hail and would lay by him. But the steamer did not return and no boat appeared, and his ship at that time demanded all his attention. Soon they lost sight of the steamer.

They lay hove to the remainder of that night and nearly all day Friday repairing the rigging, not knowing how long the ship would float. The wind had been rising all day until it was blowing a full gale, and it was difficult and dangerous work trying to replace broken masts and rigging in that rough sea. A piece of the steamer's bow still protruded from their fore chains. That afternoon they got under way again and made sail for Victoria.

Soon after dark they made out another light ahead, and this time Captain Sawyer was sure it was a lighthouse. His chart showed only one lighthouse on this part of the coast, so it could only be Cape Flattery. He bore off to the west to allow a full five miles to clear Duncan's Rock, the rock furthest off the Cape. Confident he was now in the Strait of Juan de Fuca, he relaxed for the first time since the collision and went to bed.

But at five o'clock Saturday morning, still sailing in complete darkness, fog, and rain, he was awakened when the ship scraped over a reef. Before an order could be given, her bow struck a rock and the ship began to fill. The crew lowered the boats in good order and they loaded their personal belongings and the ship's valuables and papers into them. In an hour, the sky began to lighten and they could see where they were. It didn't help. Cape Flattery was nowhere in sight, nor was the immense Strait of Fuca. They had no idea where they were.

They were in a broad bay opening to the south. The bay was dotted with rocky, tree-covered islands, islets, and shoals. Looking back along the way they had come, none of them could believe that the *Orpheus* had gotten so far before

33

striking – they had been sailing through a maze of rocks and reefs.

They were not far from a large island, and as the sea had gone down, they were able to land the captain and his family and the crew of twenty safely. But it was clear that the *Orpheus* was lost – she was jammed hard into the rocks and had filled with water. It was raining off and on, and they made tents on the beach from the ship's sails and crawled under them to wait miserably for rescue. They had no idea where they were.

The wind and rain continued on Sunday, and a strong gale blew for two days, making travel impossible. They could do nothing but forage for food and firewood. They made several trips to the wreck to salvage valuables.

On Monday, the eighth of November, a scouting party encountered an Indian encampment. The Indians explained that they were in Barclay's Sound on Vancouver Island, thirty-five miles west of Victoria. A new lighthouse had been built on Point Beale to mark the entrance to Barclay's Sound, and it was this light the *Orpheus* had seen and taken for Flattery. This light had not been on the chart they were using.

Captain Sawyer hired some of the Indians to take the first mate to Vancouver in a canoe. But the storm was still raging, and the Indians could not be induced to make the passage until the next day, when they set out in very bad conditions on Tuesday morning. Before the canoe had gotten out of Barclay's Sound and reached the open ocean, a small steamer entered the bay. It proved to be the U. S. revenue cutter *Oliver Wolcott*[9], commanded by Lieutenant Lewis Harwood.

The *Wolcott* picked up the first mate and took him back to the site of the wreck, which proved to be Copper, or

---

[9] Named for Oliver Wolcott (1726-1797), a signer of the Declaration of Independence and 19th Governor of Connecticut.

Tzartus Island, one of the Broken Group. After four days of storms and rain, Captain Sawyer's family and crew must

United States Revenue Cutter Oliver Wolcott

have been very relieved to see the steamer approaching. The cutter's crew took them aboard and took from the wreck as many valuables as they could safely retrieve, and then headed for Vancouver.

Captain Sawyer thanked Lieutenant Harwood for his rescue and remarked that it was very lucky for him that the *Wolcott* had come into such a remote bay. He asked the purpose of their visit, and only then did he learn of the greater tragedy that had taken place while he was trying to get his damaged ship to port.

Henry Jelley

Among the cabin passengers on the *Pacific* was Henry Frederick Jelley, a handsome Irishman, twenty-two years old, who had emigrated to Ontario in 1866 as a boy of thirteen. He was part of a team of surveyors hired by the Canadian Pacific Railroad to lay out routes. After a hard season of work in the remote bush, he and his friend from the survey team, A. Frazer, were heading home. Jelley was returning to his home in Ontario.

Henry F. Jelley

Now, as the *Pacific* steamed out of Esquimault, Jelley was not pleased. He had paid five dollars for a first-class cabin on the *Pacific*, but now was told he would have to sleep in a temporary berth in the saloon with twenty other men, as all the cabins were full. While his "cabin" was being banged together, he went out to walk on the deck and smoke.

A steady breeze from the southeast threw up occasional spray at the port bow, but the sea was fairly smooth. A gang of seamen was gathered around the pumps, and hoses ran up to the hurricane deck, a lighter wooden deck that sheltered the main deck and provided a place for the ship's boats. Curious, he went up the ladder and found that the crew was pumping water into the port lifeboats. An officer explained that it was to help stabilize the ship. He stepped up onto the cradle and looked down into the forward boat, which was now about half full of water. He saw that it was provided with oars, but didn't see any food or fresh water.

He went aft past the big round paddle box on the side of the ship, within which he could hear the paddles rumbling and splashing. Overhead, the massive walking beam rocked forward and back like a giant seesaw. Two seamen were playing a hosepipe into the smaller lifeboat there as well. He climbed up and found that it too was half-full, but it did not even contain oars; nor did the third and last boat.

When a knot of passengers gathered around to observe the operation, the officer asked them to go over to the port side so their weight would help level the ship. They moved across, though there was a laugh when one remarked that his mother hadn't raised him to be ballast.

Jelley examined the three boats on the starboard side and found that again, only the forward boat had oars stowed beneath the thwarts. By the time he had finished his cheroot, the officers had determined that the ship now had a list to port, and they asked the deck passengers to shift back to starboard. The sailors started pumping water into the starboard boats as well, adding to the weight above the deck level, but doing little to improve stability. These adjustments to the trim continued the whole time he was on deck. He became worried that the old steamer was not seaworthy and half-jokingly told his companion Frazer that he thought their chances of reaching San Francisco were one in a hundred. He looked to the shore and could see a carriage speeding along a coast road, and thought to himself that he would give a great deal to be on shore rather than where he was.

Eventually the sun went down and it became uncomfortably cold even in the shelter of the pilothouse. He went into the saloon and was pleased to find that the temporary berths were ready. They were rough, un-sanded and unpainted, but he didn't care. Like most of the men aboard, he was used to rough living and one night in a plank bed didn't concern him. He looked out the forward window and saw a group of men huddled in blankets in the scant shelter of the forecastle – no doubt the steerage passengers who had come aboard too late to find a dry spot inside. He felt for them, but was just happy to have a warm berth himself. He ordered a hot toddy to drive out the chill of the wind, then turned in. There was a lot of conversation and people moving about, so it was some time before he got to sleep, but he thought it was about nine o'clock.

He was awakened by a loud crash and a sharp jolt. He heard something rumbling and falling in the direction of the starboard bow. His first thought was that they had struck a rock and some broken stones had tumbled aboard, but then he decided that the shock was too slight for a grounding, or even a collision. Pulling out his pocket watch, he saw that it was nearly nine thirty. He heard the ship's bells ring to stop the engine, almost immediately followed by the signal to reverse. Perhaps they had hit some kind of flotsam; floating logs were frequently seen on this heavily-logged coast. The bells rang a third time to tell the engineer to go ahead again. Everyone jumped up and started talking at once, asking what had happened. Jelley quickly dressed and went out on deck.

It was now completely dark. The wind was still fresh, but there was little swell. He looked toward the starboard bow where the sound had come from, but could see little. He heard voices from forward say, "It is all right; we have only struck a vessel." Looking quickly around, he saw three lights some distance off the starboard beam, but he heard no one hail from either vessel.

A steward came aft and told the anxious passengers that there had been a slight collision, but the steamer was not damaged. "Do not be alarmed, ladies and gentlemen. I assure you there is no danger," he said.

Thinking the excitement was over, Jelley returned to the saloon and was preparing to return to his bed, when the ship gave a sudden lurch to port and hung there. He could clearly hear water rushing in somewhere. He hurried back out on deck along with scores of others, many in their night clothes.

Someone ran by saying, "She is making water very fast forward." Jelley went up onto the hurricane deck and went forward to the pilothouse. There he heard the Purser Mr. Hite asking Captain Howell, who was just emerging from his cabin, "Captain, what boat should I take charge of?" Jelley did not hear the answer, but realized the situation was serious. He thought of the other ship he had seen nearby.

"Captain," he asked, "are there no lights or a gun we can use for a signal?" The Captain looked around wildly.

"Yes, yes, good idea. You will find blue lights in the pilothouse." The Captain then rushed off and Jelley did not see him again. He went into the pilothouse and noticed that the engines were still running at slow ahead, though no one was at the wheel. The ship was making a slow turn to starboard.

He rummaged through the drawers and cabinets until he found six flares, and took them out onto the hurricane beck. Below him the deck was packed with terrified passengers and crew. Everyone was shouting and women and children were screaming. In his excitement, Jelley dropped one of the flares and it rolled overboard, but he crouched in the shelter of the rail and lit the fuse on the second. It gave off a brilliant white light – he had never understood why such flares were called "blue lights" – and he waved it over his head toward where the other ship had disappeared. When the flare had burned down nearly to his fingers, he tossed it overboard and lit the next. When the last sputtered out and his eyes gradually became adjusted to the dark again, he could no longer see the other ship. He went aft on the starboard side, where a number of men under the First Mate were trying to get the longboat out, but they could not do it, as the water made it too heavy to hoist out of the cradle.

Jelley ran across to see about the ship's launch on the port side, remembering that it at least contained oars. Chief Engineer Houston was in the midst of a struggling mass of people, both passengers and crew, trying to climb into it. The launch was already nearly full of people, including a dozen or so terrified women, many with children. Sitting in icy water to their waists, they were crying and calling out to their male companions who were gathered around the boat. One woman was sobbing piteously, clutching the limp body of a small boy tight in her arms. A woman beside her was crying as well, perhaps her sister, for they looked alike. Some of the women were still in their long dresses, others in robes, with their elegant hair-dos undone and their long hair plastered to their faces. Some clutched expensive furs about their shoulders. He helped five or six more ladies into the boat. At the last moment a teen-aged girl in a nightgown rushed frantically to the boat, and Jelley helped to lift her into it, very conscious of her body pressing against him through her thin nightgown. Then some of the crew pushed roughly past him and clambered into the boat as well. Mr. Houston roared at them, "Get out of there, you blackguards! This boat is for the women and children."

"We're here to protect them," cried one of the men. "We can row."

"There's not room enough for all of you! The boat's overloaded already."

"There's other men in here," replied another of the crew, pointing to several men sitting with their wives. Three of the crew seized the nearest male passenger, pulled him from the arms of his screaming wife, and threw him out of the boat, where he tumbled to the deck.

"Oh my God, save him!" cried the wife. "Please," she begged the crewmen, "for God's sake, let him back in." But they ignored her and Mr. Houston's angry bellows and set about hauling on the falls. But again they could not budge the boat. Passengers meanwhile were pressing around the launch, shouting to those within, cursing the useless crew, and impeding the gangs of men straining at the fall lines to lift the boat clear.

Mr. Houston roared out, "This boat is full! Get back, all of you, so we can launch it. There are more boats aft, on the other side."

"Those boats have already gotten off," someone shouted back. Jelley looked over the side, but could not see any boats in the water. Crowds of people on the main deck were lurching about, stumbling from one side to the other as the ship settled. Water was already pouring onto the deck through the clearing ports on the port side. He had been working to help the women, but the sight made him realize how precarious his own situation was. The steamer was settling quickly and listing farther to port. This could be the last boat.

He heard a chorus of groans and screams. Leaning over the railing, he saw water rolling over the main deck and groups of people being swept into the dark water. In seconds the water reached the hurricane deck. Jelley, clutching the gunwale, felt the boat lift from its cradle, and threw himself into it. Two or three others tumbled in on top of him.

But the boat was still tethered by its falls to the davits. Mr. Houston grabbed a fire axe from its bracket and swung it wildly three or four times, cutting the after fall. Someone else cut the bow fall and there was a ragged cheer as the launch settled into the water and drifted free of the ship. The sea was still fairly calm, and it seemed that the launch at least would survive.

But seconds later the cheer was drowned by shrieks as the steamer lurched even more precariously, leaning right above the half-swamped boat. Before anyone could get the oars into the oarlocks and pull her clear, there was a loud crack and the steamer's smokestack broke loose and toppled toward them. It clipped the gunwale of the boat, tilting it sharply to starboard, then the boat slipped free and rolled completely over to port, dumping its load into the sea.

Jelley found himself under the boat, the shock of the icy water taking his breath away. Gasping and sputtering, he clutched wildly and caught hold of the boat's gunwale. He pulled himself out from under the boat and broke the surface. Kicking frantically, he managed to pull himself up onto the upturned bottom of the boat and clutched the keel. Four other men did the same. Most of the women and children never reappeared, and the few splashing in the water, despite their piteous cries for help, were soon dragged down by their heavy waterlogged clothing. There was nothing anyone could do but to hold on desperately to the launch's keel.

Looking back, Jelley saw the steamer leaning precariously just above them, nearly on her side now. The steamer gave two or three lurches, then with a terrible rending groan, broke completely in two. Amidst the cries and screams of hundreds of men, the two halves of the *S. S. Pacific* separated and disappeared beneath the waves. The last sight he had was of the group of Chinese miners who had gathered near the smokestack with all their baggage, still crying out as the water closed over them. Everywhere he looked, men and women were struggling in the water, splashing toward anything floating. Gradually the cries for help, the heartbreaking calling of names, faded and stopped. Then all was silence.

One of the men said that a lifeboat had flotation chambers so it would not sink, even if capsized. But another said he could feel air escaping, and they could all hear it hissing out. The boat was settling and clearly would not float much longer. Jelley looked around and saw a big piece of wreckage floating nearby, with several people sitting on it. He let go and slid into the water, then struck out for it, accompanied by a miner, a large man with a full black beard. When they reached the wreckage and pulled themselves aboard, they found that it was a large piece of the hurricane deck, complete with the pilothouse, the captain's cabin just behind it, and the paddle boxes. There were now ten men and a woman on the wreckage, including Captain Howell and one of his officers, but they were as helpless as anyone else. The pilot house was the highest point, and Jelley and the miner climbed on top of it and wrapped their arms around a copper wire that ran up to the steam whistle. They crouched there, shivering, as a cold rain started.

After an interminable night, dawn finally came, but it brought a stronger wind from the southwest. Land could be seen to the east, perhaps fifteen miles away, but no sign of any vessels. They found several lifebelts floating, and used the ropes to tie themselves to the pilothouse. Two or three other rafts came in sight in the growing light, one with three men and a woman. By ten o'clock the wind and sea had so increased that the raft began to go to pieces, and finally a portion of the deck with the paddle boxes broke away. The Captain and the other survivors lay partly awash on the deck as it drifted away, clinging wordlessly to whatever handholds they could find.

Now it was just Jelley and the miner on the pilothouse. The raft broke again and the pilothouse went to pieces, but they still clung to the roof. By the afternoon the wind had risen to a full gale and the seas were running "as high as mountains," as Jelley described it. Wave after wave swept over them, making it difficult just to breathe. When he felt he had the strength, Jelley pulled himself to his feet to look for rescue. Once his heart leaped when he saw something not far away, but then he realized it was the hurricane deck raft again. The two groups signaled to each other, but could do no more than hold on. They saw other pieces of wreckage with people huddled on them.

Sometime around noon a column of smoke was seen in the south, raising all their spirits. As it came closer, they could make out a northbound steamer coming toward them. Captain Howell recognized it as the *S. S. California*, the

43

other ship owned by Goodall, Nelson, and Perkins. She steamed past at two or three miles distance, but for all their shouting and waving, it hurried past and disappeared over the horizon. Another ship was spotted in the distance, but it never came close.

Around two in the afternoon, a shout went up from one of the other rafts. A sail had been spotted, tacking in toward the coast and coming toward them. Jelley stood up and waved and they all shouted. But then the ship tacked and headed back out to sea. Soon she was gone. The miner lost all heart at this. Jelley tried to cheer him and encourage him to hold out, but about four o'clock, unable to hold his head out of the water, the man drowned by his side. Now, with the body of his only companion floating against him with every wave, the weather worsening, and the temperature falling, Jelley began to lose heart himself. The sun went down and with it all hope of rescue that day. He could barely stand the thought of another night in the water. He spent the long hours talking to his dead companion, debating which of them had it worse.

Cape Flattery lighthouse was now clearly visible, its comforting beam sweeping across the heaving ocean, taunting him with its promise of life and warmth. The storm grew worse; heavy rain poured down and the waves frequently submerged him completely. In one such wave, he felt himself sliding across the raft and clutched wildly at a handhold. His lashings had worn through from the constant friction against the rough broken wood. His legs too were being painfully scraped and bruised. His fingers were so frozen and swollen now, he knew he wouldn't be able to hold on to the raft. With apologies to his companion, he untied him, rolled him off the raft, and used his ropes to fix himself more securely. By the time he was done, the body had floated away.

He drifted northward close to Cape Flattery and thought for a while he might come ashore there, but then a strong current coming out of the Strait carried him away from the cape and toward the southern shore of Vancouver Island. The sun came up around eight o'clock on Saturday morning. When he raised his head to look around, the first rays of sunshine were lighting the sails of a large ship coming toward him. He tried to stand, but his frozen legs would not function. He pulled himself up to a sitting position and waved. He tried to shout, but his voice was little more than a croak.

But it was clear the vessel had seen him. It hove to and lowered a boat. They tied lines to the raft, then cut his lashings and lifted him gently into the boat. Someone wrapped him in a blanket. When he was lifted aboard the ship, the captain leaned over him and handed him a whiskey.

"You're aboard the *Messenger*[10] out of Boston, son," he said. "I'm Captain Gilkey[11]. Who the hell are you?"

"Henry Jelley," he croaked, the whiskey burning like hot acid in his throat. "Steamship *Pacific*. Sank Thursday evening."

"God preserve us. It's nine-thirty Saturday morning. And you've been floating for all that time, in that storm – on that scrap of wood?" he asked, pointing to the little raft as the men hoisted it dripping onto the foredeck.

At that same moment the crew of the *Orpheus* was clambering ashore in Barclay Sound, not thirty miles away.

---

[10] The *Messenger* was a famous and successful extreme clipper ship built by Jacob Bell in New York in 1852. She was condemned in Mauritius in 1879.

[11] Captain Isaac F. Gilkey (1838-1904) was born in Searsport, Maine and was a captain by age 25. He commanded numerous ships and traded around the world. He died in 1904, aged 66.

Neil Henley

While it had taken Henry Jelley some time to discover that the steamer was in danger, for quartermaster Neil Henley, asleep in his berth in the forecastle, there was no mystery at all. He was awoken by a tremendous crash that threw him from his bunk. He landed in a foot of water, with a powerful stream pouring in through the splintered hull planks beside his berth. The entire bow of the ship was open. Henley did not

Neil O. Henley

try to grab his belongings or anything he might need. His only thought was to get out of the ship before it went down.

He scrambled to the ladder and swarmed up it, the water rising around his waist. He threw open the scuttle and plunged into a throng of panicked people. People were shouting and racing in every direction, shoving others out of their way. Henley joined them, bouncing from person to person. But now he had a purpose – to reach the hurricane deck and the life boats. He was not alone, and the ladders to the boat deck were a solid mass of shoving, desperate people. There was nothing to do but to join them and allow himself to be shoved up the stairs along with everyone else. Most turned aft to the where the nearest lifeboats were, but Henley squeezed between the top of the paddle box and the structure surrounding the walking beam, which was still rising and falling as usual. He made for the pilothouse to ask the captain what he should do. When he went in, he heard the captain shouting, "Hard a-starboard![12] Fast as you can, man!"

The ship responded very sluggishly to the wheel, but slowly fell off the wind and turned to port. The rising seas pushed her bow around until she lay parallel to the seas. They were no longer pounding into her wounded bow, but they caused a severe roll that sent the old hull groaning and people staggering.

Henley peered out into the dark to starboard and saw the lights of a large sailing ship. The green starboard light was very close, but she was veering away and swiftly moving off.

"Rammed us, by damn, the blasted fool!" growled the captain. "Does anyone know how bad it is?"

"The whole bow's gone, skipper," said Henley. She's all tore open. She's going down."

"God help us all. Abandon ship! Tell the engine room. Every man to the boats. Each officer will take charge of one boat. Women and children first, then the male passengers. Except for those officers, no member of the crew is to board a boat until all passengers are safely launched, is that understood?"

The half-dozen men in the pilothouse nodded, but each was well aware that there were not enough boats for this number of passengers.

The Captain and his officers went out to the starboard side. Henley and the quartermaster from the helm started aft on the port side and met the Chief Engineer just reaching the boat deck. His eyes were wild. "Fires are out. Water's over the boiler already," he gasped. "Hope it don't blow."

"Captain's orders, Mr. Houston. Each senior officer to a boat," Henley told him. "Women and children first, no crew

---

[12] Until the 1930's, helm directions were always given as if steering by tiller. Thus "Hard a-starboard" meant to turn to port, or the left.

to board while there are still passengers aboard." Houston stared a moment, taking it in, then nodded. "Who's is this boat?" he asked, pointing to the longboat.

"I... I don't know," Henley stammered. "The captain didn't assign them."

"Right, then. This one is mine. You'll help the women into the boat and keep everybody else out. Got it? There may be trouble, so round up any help you see."

Henley started aft but was confronted by an approaching group of terrified women, many herding small children. The leading one, carrying a boy of one or two, clutched his arm.

"They said the boats are up here," she said, already shivering against the cold.

"Yes, ma'am. There's one right behind me. We'll get you all off, but I need some help." He spotted a few faces he recognized in the group of men pressing in behind the women. "You seamen, come for'ard. Everyone, let those men through."

Everyone was talking at once, asking what had happened, whether they were sinking, were there enough boats, how far they were from shore. He had no answers, but everyone could see the steamer was going down. Each wave was pouring over her sides as she rolled, and she had a decided list to port.

Three seamen forced their way through the crowd and joined him. "Stay here," Henley told them. "Let them through one at a time. Women and children first."

He returned to the boat, where Mr. Houston was casting off the last lashings. "Gott in Himmel, it's half full of water," he cried. "What were you lot doing up here – going swimming?"

"It was ballast. We had a bad list."

"Well, it was a damned stupid idea. Even if we swim around in there and pull the plug, it will take a half hour to drain it."

Their discussion was cut short as five or six women and several children appeared. They looked at Mr. Houston, clearly grateful to see an officer in charge. "What do we do?" asked one.

"Well, we'll get you in the boat, then the men will lower it. It should be safe enough, ladies. We'll all be fine. There is one problem, though. The boat was some water in it."

"The ship is sinking, sir," replied one woman. "Do you think we are worried about wet hems?"

"No, ma'am. But it's rather a lot of water." He helped her step up on the cradle, then lifted her as if he were putting her aboard a horse. She looked down at the water sloshing over the thwarts.

"Ah, yes," she said. "I see what you mean." She gently lowered herself onto the thwart, with water sloshing around her hips. She gasped at the cold. Many of the women were reluctant to get into the water and some of the children started screaming, but there was nothing for it. Henley and a male passenger started lifting women up into the boat and then passing them their children.

It went smoothly for a few minutes, but then the steamer gave another lurch, and everything broke down. The seamen posted at the paddle box came running, followed by an angry, frightened mob of passengers, pushing and fighting each other to reach the boat. Mr. Houston roared out orders, but no one paid him any attention. Husbands started lifting their wives into the boat, then clambering in after them.

"Let her through, let her through, God damn you!" a powerful voice roared. Henley recognized the voice of a sea captain, trained to be heard at the mast head in a hurricane. It was Captain Parsons, leading his wife and her sister through the crowd, shoving men roughly aside. His wife was holding a small boy in her arms. When they reached the boat, Henley helped Mrs. Parsons in, while Captain Parsons bent to pick up the boy. Just then several men lunged out of the crowd and tried to climb aboard, elbowing Captain

Parsons out of their way. Parsons stumbled and dropped the boy, who started to wail. The men already in the boat stood up and shoved the newcomers violently back. One large man toppled from the gunwale, arms flailing. He landed right on the top of the Parsons boy, whose crying instantly ceased. Parsons rolled the man aside and knelt by his son's side, but the boy's head was twisted to one side; he was clearly dead. Mrs. Parsons screamed, "My boy! My boy! Give him to me, Otis." Dumbly, hardly knowing what he did, Captain Parsons picked up the little limp body and passed it to his mother. Mrs. Parsons and her sister were both sobbing. The crowd looked on in horror, shocked into near silence.

Then the crewmen standing nearby took advantage of the pause. They suddenly rushed the boat and clambered in. The Chief Engineer roared at them to get out, but they refused, and even tore one man from the arms of his wife and threw him from the boat. It was terrible to see the desperation on everyone's face. At the last minute a young girl came rushing out of the crowd and a male passenger hoisted her into the boat, then, taking one quick look at the advancing water, threw himself in after her.

At that moment the water flooded across the hurricane deck, swirling about their ankles. The boat lifted from its cradle and floated, but the falls were still attached at bow and stern. Mr. Houston used a fire axe to cut the stern fall. One of the seamen seized the axe and swung out from the davit to cut the bow fall, and the boat started to drift away. But then the ship lurched to port. Her smokestack broke off and crashed into a mass of men already struggling in the water. The splash threw the boat against the side of the sinking ship, and it quickly rolled over amid the screams of the women and children.

Helpless to save them, Henley clung to a chain railing as the water rose around his waist. Then he was floating, and the sinking steamer pulled him under as she plunged toward the bottom. The chain slipped from his fingers and he was pushed back to the surface by a bubble of air that rose from the ship. He struck around wildly until his fingers struck something. It was one of the hurricane deck skylights. Dazed, he clung to the skylight for what he thought was ten minutes, until the seas capsized the skylight and broke his grip. He saw a larger piece of wreckage not far away with several people clinging to it. He let go and swam over to it. When he caught the edge, a man reached down and pulled him onto the wreckage. It was a large piece of the hurricane deck, complete with the pilot-house and part of the paddle box, which had been torn off as the steamer went under. There were nine men and one woman on it. Looking around, Henley saw no trace of the steamer or any boats, just a shouting, screaming mass of people thrashing in the water.

Within minutes the terrible cries diminished until, one by one, they fell silent. Then it was just the raft drifting in silence. Captain Howell was there, and the second mate Mr. Wells, plus the second cook Holdsworth, another quartermaster, and three passengers, one a young woman named Miss Reynolds of San Francisco. A few moments later two men swam up and joined them, one of whom he recognized as Mr. Jelley who had gone in the launch. Mr. Wells said that he thought the first mate, Mr. McDonaugh, had gotten off safely with the longboat and the quarter boat under Assistant Engineer D. M. Bassett may have gotten away as well, though no one on the raft had actually seen any boats floating after the wreck.

They all clung there in silence, each lost in his own misery. Some held to the steamer's wheel, others to handles in the cabin; they used the broken tiller ropes to tie themselves to the raft. The wind continued to build until it was blowing a fresh gale. The seas rose accordingly, each trying to pull them from the deck. At one point the raft broke in two, Mr. Jelley and another passenger drifting away with the pilothouse, the rest of them clinging to the paddle box.

At one A.M on Friday, a large sea swept completely over the raft and tore them all from their grips. Only the ropes kept them from being lost.

Around four in the morning, the biggest sea yet broke over the raft, carrying away the screaming Miss Reynolds. The second officer Mr. Wells, who had been talking to the girl throughout to keep up her spirits, immediately untied himself and swam after her. He caught her and dragged her back to the raft. With Henley's help they managed to get her back aboard, but after that she seemed to lose all hope. Her strength quickly waned, and after a time she lay senseless on the deck, the waves streaming her long hair from one side to the other. Sometime later another wave swept over them, and the woman was no longer there. Mr. Wells again plunged in after her, but this time he did not return.

Henley drifted in a half-conscious state, the cold making him dull and sluggish. Everything passed as if in a dream. At first light on Friday they found that two of the men were gone as well. No one had seen them go overboard. Now it was just the Captain, Holdsworth, Henley, and a miner, whose name Henley never learned.

At nine A. M. the cook Holdsworth died and was cast adrift. Later in the afternoon the weather cleared and they could see land about fifteen miles to the east and other survivors clinging to wreckage. A sailing vessel appeared in the distance but turned away before they could be seen. The raft drifted north past Cape Flattery light. Around five P. M. a large empty dry-goods box floated near and Henley was able to catch hold of it and haul it aboard. He crawled inside and it gave him some minimal protection at last from the wind. The sun went down, but the wind and seas remained very high throughout the long night. When dawn came on Saturday, their hopes were again raised that they might be rescued, but the long day passed without a single sight of a ship. The miner was washed away during the afternoon, leaving just Captain Howell and Henley to face the long night alone.

Sunday morning the storm continued, and they were continually thrown against the raft by the waves sweeping over it. Finally the Captain succumbed and was washed overboard, leaving Henley alone and barely alive. The current was carrying him into the Strait of Fuca, and he could see Vancouver Island to the north, though he was closer to the Washington shore. Still no vessels appeared. He drifted into a mass of floating kelp, which calmed the seas and he could at last fall asleep for four hours. He felt neither hunger nor thirst. He drifted throughout that long day and into Sunday night.

At three A.M Monday morning he heard a noise that was neither wind nor waves and poked his head out of his box. There, only a few hundred yards away, was the light of a steamer. A boat was moving slowly through the kelp. He shouted as loudly as he could, and they took him aboard and gave him every comfort they could offer. The steamer proved to be the United States Revenue cutter *Oliver Wolcott*, Lieutenant Harwood. Neil Henley had been in the icy water for seventy-eight hours – three and a half days.

The *Wolcott* circled the area searching for other survivors or wreckage, but did not sight any. Lieutenant Harwood turned west to Neah Bay, just inside the strait on the Washington side. As they approached Waddah Island, which is just off the bay, they recovered the body of a man wearing a lifebelt. They found a letter from his sister in his pocket, identifying him as Robert Jones, a Welshman from the town of Rhyl in the north of Wales. Henley identified him as the second steward of the *Pacific*.

They docked at Neah Bay and Henley was put into the charge of Mr. Huntington, the Indian agent there, who cared for him kindly and tended his wounds.

Aftermath

The *Wolcott* went right back to sea, cruising along the coast of Vancouver Island. They took Indians and canoes with them to search along the shore where their boats could not reach. The *Wolcott* picked up two trunks, one of which was a lady's with valuable wearing apparel and children's clothing. On the outside of it was a leather tag marked, "Mrs. W. Lawson, Bank of British North America, San Francisco." The other trunk contained circus props, straps, and horse harness, and was evidently the trunk of Mr. Hurlburt, the horse trainer. Two days later the *Wolcott* found the wrecked *Orpheus*. The pilot boat from Neah Bay also went out to search, as well as a British tugboat.

Tuesday morning, the 9th, the steamer *Gussie Telfair* arrived at Neah Bay and reported seeing a disabled ship near Cape Flattery on Friday with a broken bowsprit and flying the flag upside down, a signal of distress. The *Telfair* was unable to assist due to the conditions and lost sight of the other ship. This was presumed to be the *Orpheus*. When they learned of the loss of the *Pacific*, they went back out immediately and searched the Washington shore as far as Quillayute, forty miles south of Cape Flattery. They stopped at each Indian settlement and asked the inhabitants to search the shore for bodies or wreckage. The steamers spoke to several vessels but none had seen anything of the disabled vessel. The *Telfair* found three bodies floating off Cape Flattery, one of which was a woman with a ring marked "L. and H.," supposed to be Mrs. Kellar, a tourist returning to San Francisco. Also recovered was the body of George T. Vining of Puyallup, who had on his person bills of lading for hops shipped by him at Tacoma. The watch found on him stopped at 9:30 p. m. on the night of the disaster. The other body was evidently a fireman or coal passer but could not be identified. All three were wearing life preservers. On Thursday the 11th, the *Telfair* returned with the bodies. Three weeks later the *Gussie Telfair* would strike a rock and sink, but without the loss of life.

Tuesday evening the bark *Arkwright* arrived at Neah Bay from Nanaimo on Vancouver. Her Captain Marshall made this report:

> "Sunday, November 7th, off Neah Bay, Straits of Fuca, passed a steamer's house, life buoys, cargo, gangways, furniture, trunks, gun carriage, doors grained inside and painted white outside, part of paddle-box and numerous other pieces of wreck of all descriptions; two hours later passed close alongside the body of a woman, floating with a life-preserver attached and clothed with nothing but a single undergarment; the body was apparently that of a large, middle-aged woman, with a heavy head of brown hair; could not see the face, as it floated downward; knew the debris and body came from some steamer wrecked near-by; looked for further indications of the wreck, but coming on dark and blowing hard saw nothing more. Concluded the steamer had foundered or gone ashore during the heavy gale of the 5th or 6th of November, which I experienced outside Cape Flattery, and was obliged to run in the Straits for shelter, it blowing fearfully from S. W. and a heavy sea running, and so thick and rainy that I could not see the land a quarter of a mile distant. When I was running in I passed Flattery not over two miles off, and could hear nothing of a steam-whistle, and know it was not sounded

the five hours I was in hearing. Such neglect, in all probability, largely contributed toward the loss of the steamer, and for common humanity's sake I think such often-repeated acts of neglect on the part of those in charge of lighthouses on this coast should not go unpunished."

Distraught relatives were wiring the authorities, begging that the search not be abandoned. There was still hope that a boat or two had survived, or that survivors had reached shore and might be suffering. The *Wolcott* went out again. This time she:

"followed the shore line of the south side of the Straits, starting at Point Wilson and searching every floating object, and landing boats at different places where there was a probability of a drift lodging, and requesting residents and lighthouse tenders all along the route to keep a good look out and report anything that might be of interest. A number of Indian canoes were overhauled above Port Angeles, who reported that a board having on it some writing pertaining to a wreck had been picked up at Eiwab, but on arriving at that place the surf ran high, and it was impossible to land a boat. Neither would any canoes come off from the shore, although they were repeatedly hailed. Light portions of the wreck were found on the south shore, as far west as Freshwater Bay; then all indications disappeared, and Captain Harwood on Sunday morning headed the cutter for the Vancouver shore around Sooke and Beecher Bay. The water was covered with floating kelp and pieces of the wreck. About noon a body was discovered with a life preserver around it. On getting aboard it proved to be that of a man about forty years of age, about five feet six inches high, black hair and beard, and dressed in a dark tweed suit. On his body was found an American silver watch, and in a body belt $97 in coin, and notes from his diary and a steamer ticket. His name was discovered to be D. C. McIntyre. He had been up on the Frazer River since September last, and had arrived in Victoria just previous to the sailing of the *Pacific*. A receipt for a poll tax paid in Jefferson District, Sutter County, California, was also found, and it appeared that he had resided at Marysville, California, for some time. He came there direct from the East and had been employed by Reuben Hobbs, and it is probable that some of his friends or relatives may reside at Marysville. His body was taken to Port Townsend and will be buried there. The steamer *Los Angeles* was spoken Sunday afternoon, but reported seeing only some light portions of the wreck on her way up the Straits. Nothing was left undone by Captain Harwood that would render the search effective and complete, and to convey to the friends of the victims news of their sad fate. Many telegrams were received from different parts of the coast containing a description of persons who had sailed on the Pacific, but there is little hope of any further discoveries of living or dead victims of the sad calamity."

The following Sunday, Judge Horten of Port Angeles, well inside the Straits, discovered the body of a man in a bad state of preservation. His linen was marked "E. L. H." and he had a diamond ring on his finger. He was identified as Mr. Everett L. Hastings, of Crane & Hastings, brewers, of San Francisco.

On Wednesday, November 24th, a British tugboat arrived from San Juan Island with two more bodies. One was identified as Mrs. G. W. Lawson of Victoria, wife of the Honorable G. W. Lawson, a legislator in British Columbia. The other was that of a young woman that had been discovered by Indians of Beechy Head and turned over to the U. S. Garrison on San Juan Island. It had on a life-preserver marked "*Pacific.*" From the dress, the indications were that she had to leave the ship in haste. The body was identified as that of the young school teacher, Miss Fanny Palmer, whose mother had such forebodings of her death. The girl's body had washed up within a mile of her home. Bits of her luggage were found on both the Canadian and Washington sides of the strait. A few days later, a school friend of Fanny's received a letter Fanny had written and posted just before she boarded the *Pacific*, in which she said she had premonitions that she would not survive the trip.

One day some Beechy Head Indians arrived in the harbor in a canoe, towing another canoe in which was the body of a large man. The body was recognized as the remains of John Howe Sullivan, the Cassiar Gold Commissioner, who had sailed with hopes of soon being back with his friends in Ireland, and spending the Christmas holiday with them. In his pockets were found a considerable sum in drafts and gold, a gold watch and chain, and a pocket diary. In the diary, evidently written just before he went to bed, was this entry:

"Left Victoria for old Ireland on Thursday, 4th, about noon. Some of the miners drunk;

some ladies sick; feel sorry at temporarily leaving a country in which I have lived so long; spent last evening at dear old Hillside."

News of the wreck continued to come in sporadically; this item bringing further pain to the friends of Sue Moody:

"About a month after the ship had gone down, and when the first burst of grief had been replaced by a feeling of resignation, and while the shores were still patrolled for many miles in the hope of finding more bodies, a man walking along the southern face of Beacon Hill observed a fragment of wreckage lying high and dry on the beach. Upon examination it proved to be part of a stateroom stanchion or support, and on its white surface were written in bold business hand, in pencil, these words:

S.P. MOODY. ALL LOST

The handwriting was identified as that of S. P. Moody, the principal owner of the Moodyville sawmills, who was a passenger. It is supposed that when he found the ship was going down and no hope remained of saving his life, Mr. Moody wrote this message from the sea on the stanchion in the faint hope that it might someday be picked up and his fate known. This hope was not in vain, and I believe the piece of wreckage with the inscription upon it is still cherished by the Moody family."

Rather than taking the time to write the message while trying to escape the sinking ship, it is more likely that the stanchion was part of a piece of wreckage to which Moody and other survivors clung. When he found he was alone and his grip fading, he left this poignant message.

The rudder of the *Pacific* came ashore in perfect condition near Race Rocks, and in the immediate vicinity large quantities of the deck, state rooms, and hurricane deck floated on shore. Only one other body was ever recovered, that of Thomas J. Farrell of Victoria. Of the rest, or even their number, nothing is known.

A coroner's inquest was held in Victoria on November 11th on the body of passenger Thomas Ferrell. The jury took only three hours to reach their verdict:

"That the body is that of Thomas J. Farrell; that the said Thos. J. Farrell came to his death by drowning; that the said Thos. J. Farrell was a passenger on board the American steamship *Pacific*, which sailed from Victoria, B. C., for San Francisco on the 4th of November, 1875; that the said steamship *Pacific* sank after a collision with the American ship *Orpheus*, off Cape Flattery, on the night of the 4th of November. 1875; that the *Pacific* struck the *Orpheus* on the starboard side with her stem a very light blow, the shock of which should not have damaged the *Pacific*, if a sound and substantial vessel; that the collision between the *Pacific* and the *Orpheus* was caused by the *Orpheus* not keeping the approaching *Pacific's* light on the port bow, as when first seen, but putting the helm to starboard and unjustifiably crossing the *Pacific's* bow. That the watch on deck of the *Pacific* at the time of the collision was not sufficient in number to keep a proper lookout, the said watch consisting only of three men, namely, one at the wheel, one supposed to be on lookout, and the third mate, a young man of doubtful experience. The *Pacific* had about 238 persons on board at the time of the collision. That the *Pacific* had five boats, whose utmost carrying capacity did not exceed 160 persons. That the boats were not and could not be lowered by the undisciplined and insufficient crew. That the captain of the *Orpheus* sailed away after the collision, and did not remain by the *Pacific* to ascertain the amount of damage she had sustained."

An inquest was also held in San Francisco to determine the cause of the accident, but it was universally criticized. The government officials in charge were the same Inspector of Hulls and the Inspector of Boilers who had certified the *Pacific* as seaworthy just months before her last voyage. They were not likely to conclude that the disaster was due to their own incompetence. The inquest was also held behind closed doors, with the public and reporters excluded. Finally, the results were never made public and no one was ever charged – not the officers or owners, and certainly not the two inspectors. The owners of the two ships were never required to pay any damages to the families of those who had died.

Most people blamed Captain Sawyer of the *Orpheus* for callously sailing away and leaving hundreds of people to drown. Captain Sawyer claimed he had thought his own ship was sinking and had no time to wonder about the steamer. But some of his own crew claimed that he had been drunk; others said he was lost and had hoped to speak with the steamer to learn his position.

The Sacramento *Daily Union*, while agreeing the primary blame was Sawyer's, excoriated the inquest for finding no fault with the *Pacific's* captain and owners:

> "The condemnation of the *Orpheus*, however, cannot exonerate the *Pacific*. In her case the conditions appear to have been singularly marked by recklessness. Such an arrangement as that all the crew should turn in at night, leaving only three men on deck, was surely never before heard of on a passenger vessel, and it is not less to the purpose that the crew appear to have been good-for-nothing when they did turn out. As to the question of the steamer's unseaworthiness, we think it perfectly obvious that the Coroner's jury are right in asserting that the shock of the blow she sustained "could not have injured the *Pacific*, if a sound and substantial vessel." Messrs. Goodall & Nelson may protest as much as they please, but they cannot protest away the ugly fact that their vessel did break to pieces and go to the bottom after a collision which, judging from

its effect upon the ship she ran into, ought not to have started a single butt, not to speak of opening the timber ends at her stem and breaking her back into the bargain. The truth is that she could hardly have sunk quicker if she had been built of glass.

"A greater outrage than this sham inquiry, conducted in secret by the officials who are mainly responsible for the disaster, was never heard of, and an American public is the only one in the civilized world that would tamely submit to it, if we may judge from the way the people behave elsewhere under similar circumstances. In striking contrast to this shameful farce has been the conduct of the Victoria people and authorities. There they held an inquest, brought the ablest counsel to examine witnesses, put veteran seamen on the jury, and dragged the facts to light, regardless where the responsibility might be made to rest. Not content with this, the Grand Jury took the matter up, and made a most able and vigorous presentment of it, suggesting to the Government precautionary measures which, if adopted, will make similar hideous sacrifices of life impossible in the future.

"It appears to have been thought in some quarters that a stand might confidently be made on the assumption of her seaworthiness, it being supposed that she had gone to the bottom, and that no evidence could ever be adduced in refutation of that theory. The forces of nature, however, have been fighting against the greed and brutality of sordid ship-owners, and her timbers, washed ashore on Vancouver Island, now offer incontestable proof that she was fit for nothing but to be pulled to pieces for the sake of her metal. It is reported that these timbers are in such a condition that they will not bear handling, but actually fall to pieces with their own weight, when lifted. Against such damning testimony the assertions of Messrs. Goodall & Nelson will have little weight, even though they should be backed by the certificates of every Federal Inspector of Boilers in the United States."

Captain Sawyer was reviled on all sides. When seven of his crew testified that he had been drunk throughout the voyage and deliberately ran his ship ashore, a warrant was issued for his arrest. On December 31, Sawyer fled the country, taking passage on the steamship *Colorado* for Panama. The U. S. Marshal said Sawyer had deceived him about his intentions, but Sawyer's remaining friends asserted that he had been perfectly open about his plans to leave the country. The marshal wired to San Diego to have Sawyer arrested, but the telegram did not arrive in time. A few months later, Captain Sawyer and his wife sailed from Panama to Calcutta, where all trace of them is lost.

The Responsibility

There is plenty of blame to be spread around.

Captain Robert Waterman[13], the Inspector of Hulls in San Francisco, certified the *Pacific* as seaworthy when she was clearly barely afloat. He also presided at the secret inquiry and absolved himself, the owners, and indeed everyone, of any blame.

Captain Robert Waterman

The *Pacific's* owners Charles Goodall, Christopher Nelson, and George Perkins were operating a very old ship that had been sunk once, been abandoned to rot twice, and declared unfit for service. They directed their officers and agents to pack as many passengers aboard as possible to maximize their profits.

Captain Howell allowed a number of passengers aboard that he knew to be unsafe and beyond his ship's certification. He knew the boats were inadequate in number and condition and were not provisioned and supplied for use. He had the life boats filled with water to trim the ship, rather than shift

---

[13] Captain Robert Waterman (1808-1884) was a prominent sea captain and the founder of the cities of Fairfield and Cordelia, California. He set three sailing speed records; his time of 74 days from Hong Kong to New York City has never been bettered in a sail-powered vessel. He was reputed as a martinet, and was once convicted of assault against a crewman in a controversial California criminal case.

cargo and ballast as should have been done. He knew the crew was not trained in emergency procedures.

There were allegations in the *Portland Oregonian* that Captain Howell had been drunk. The evidence given for this claim was an occurrence that happened the day before the fatal passage, when the *Pacific* was at Tacoma. She was advertised to leave at noon, but Captain Howell complained of a headache and remained in his cabin, giving orders he was not to be disturbed until he awoke. So the *Pacific*, with passengers and mail aboard and with steam up, waited at the dock all afternoon and did not leave for Victoria until that evening.

But there had never before been complaints of drunkenness against Captain Howell, and several of his friends wrote letters saying that he did not drink immoderately. Two men who dined with him the evening before they left Victoria testified that he was not drunk that night. One, A. J. Edwards, wrote to the *Oregonian* with more indignation than grammar: "From my own knowledge I say it is Wholely untreu and the *Oregonian* will be held responcible until the name of the Wrighter is published. The evidence of all those who knew him Say that more officiant or better qualified officer Does not Live."

First Officer McDonaugh did not stand his assigned watch and left the deck in the hands of an inexperienced officer. He allowed the deck crew to go to their berths when they should have been on watch. Everyone must have known that this was both irresponsible and illegal. Captain Howell might have known of the arrangement; perhaps he even ordered it; we cannot know. But it was the responsibility of the other officers, or even a seaman like Henley, to go to the captain and let him know that regulations were being flaunted. All were complicit, but ultimately the captain is responsible for the actions and inactions of his officers and crew.

The *Pacific's* crew were undisciplined and untrained. They disobeyed direct orders and rushed the boats, throwing out passengers to make room for themselves. They were certainly responsible for many of the deaths. But it must be acknowledged that, even had the boats floated and been adequately provided, with that many people and an undisciplined, mutinous crew, they could never have survived the severe gale that lashed the coast for the next three days. They were doomed from the start.

Nevertheless, some scores of people survived the sinking and found wreckage to support them for several days. If any of the three vessels that passed within sight had kept a better lookout, they might have been rescued. The *SS California* passed close enough to be recognized by Captain Howell from his raft.

Did the lighthouse keepers on Cape Flattery see nothing of the drama on their horizon, the "blue lights" shown by the *Pacific*, or the wreckage with survivors that floated past the island? Was the light out during the storm Friday night as Captain Sawyer claimed, dooming the *Orpheus*? Were the fog signals sounded?

Captain Sawyer of the *Orpheus* was (and still is) considered the primary cause of the disaster. His crew asserted that he was drunk throughout the voyage, and that he was lost and had deliberately approached the steamer to learn his position, bringing the vessels dangerously close in poor conditions and without signaling his intent. He denied these charges. But he did cross the path of the *Pacific* and come to a stop, violating the rules of navigation. He also left the scene without ascertaining if the steamer were in danger. He claimed he was more concerned about his own ship, but his was the heavier and more strongly-built vessel. It was reasonable to assume the steamer might have been badly damaged.

Gilbert, Sawyer's helmsman that night, testified that after the collision, the *Orpheus'* carpenter examined the hold and determined that the ship was not making water, and Captain Sawyer ordered the ship to get under way. This happened less than five minutes after the collision, and Gilbert testified the steamer was then two miles off and in clear sight. The crew of the *Orpheus* heard Captain Howell call "Ship Ahoy!" three times and reported it to their captain, but he turned and went away. Many of the *Pacific's* passengers were still alive at this time and might have been picked up. It is a master's legal duty to render aid to survivors if it does not increase the danger to his own vessel.

Captain Sawyer is almost certainly the cause of the destruction of the *Pacific*. He is unquestionably responsible for the later loss of his own ship. To be sailing free with all plain sails set when he is in proximity to a coast and his position is unknown is irresponsible at best. He was more than thirty-five miles from his dead reckoning position, and his claim that the Cape Flattery light was not lit is not supported by any other reports. Though it is true that the Point Beale light that he mistook for the Cape was not on his chart, he is responsible for carrying current charts. The light had been established sixteen months before.

Whether his crew was correct in claiming that he was drunk and intentionally drove the *Orpheus* aground will never be known. The disaster and the tremendous loss of life stirred strong emotions that lasted for decades, and the people howled for someone to blame. Public opinion and press coverage of him was vitriolic. His precipitate flight is suspicious, but barratry – the deliberate destruction by a captain of the vessel under his command – was still a capital offense. Knowing he could be hanged, any man might decide to absent himself.

EPILOG

After Neil Henley recovered from his injuries, he remained in Victoria and worked at the Royal Hotel, then he went to San Francisco. He was hired again by the Goodall, Nelson and Perkins Steamship Company and sailed on their vessels for fifteen months. He then became quartermaster on the Revenue Cutter *Corwin* in Alaska for two years. He tried mining in the Cassiar gold fields but was not successful. In 1880, he moved to Port Townsend and joined the crew of the Revenue Cutter *Oliver Wolcott* that had rescued him. In 1883, he moved to Steilacoom, Washington, was a town marshal, and worked as a prison guard at the McNeil Island Federal Penitentiary. On the last day of 1885 he married Marcella Digby and they eventually had seven children.

During the Spanish-American War, Henley returned to sea as quartermaster aboard a troop transport in the Philippine Islands. In 1899, he returned to McNeil Island and built boats for the penitentiary. He became Captain Henley, Superintendent of Boats, a position he held for 22 years until he retired in 1921. He died at age 86 in 1944 and is buried in Tacoma.

Henry Jelley had been returning to Ontario when he left the Cassiar fields and boarded the *Pacific*. After giving testimony in both Victoria and San Francisco, he resumed his journey and returned to the family farm in Port Stanley on Lake Erie. Later he sailed to Ireland and got married, then returned to Port Stanley where he farmed and engaged in commercial fishing. Jelley, age 77, died in Canada in 1930.

The great white stallion Mazeppa was found floating in the Strait a week or so after the wreck. He was saddled and bridled, which would never have been done while he was in his stall for the passage. It is assumed that some member of the Hurlburt troupe found time to go down into the hold, saddle and bridle the horse, and somehow get him on deck. Whether it was a valiant attempt to save the horse, or in hopes of riding the horse to shore, will never be known.

Twenty-five years after the wreck, in December 1900, the Hibernia Bank of San Francisco was closing out inactive accounts and found an account containing $47,000 registered in the name of Jennie Mandeville, the famous singer who died on the *Pacific*. The money was turned over to a public administrator named Freese, who advertised to try to locate the next of kin. Eventually he contacted William and Beatrice States, the children of Jennie's sister Agatha. All the rest of the Mandeville family were dead. But at the hearing to confer the money to the heirs, a woman named Minnie Adams Brooks arrived from Chicago and said the money was hers. She said that before Jenny married Captain Parsons she was secretly married in 1847 to an actor in New York named George Adams. Minnie was their daughter and had been raised by a woman named Hoag. She had several letters between Jenny Mandeville and Mrs. Hoag, as well as a marriage certificate of the earlier marriage and her own baptismal certificate, all confirming her story. The States said they knew nothing of such a marriage and doubted the story. But then Minnie Brooks produced a remarkable document.

She said that at the time of the disaster she was married to a man named Bowdish. A fortnight after the accident that killed her mother a letter was delivered to her. It said that a bottle had been found by a United States coast guard on November 15, 1875, on the beach at Cape Flattery. In this bottle was a letter addressed thus: "To Whoever Finds This: Please forward to Mrs. Minnie Bowdish, San Francisco, Calif." The letter read as follows:

70

On board steamer *Pacific*,
November 4, 1875, 6 p.m.

My Precious Child,

We are in awful peril, with little hope, unless some vessel comes to our relief soon. I know there is one chance that some of the hardy ones of this ship may be picked up in the event of our going down. Therefore. I have given five letters to men who can swim. They are friends of ours from Victoria, and will mail the letters if they live. This one I put in a bottle and drop into the care of the sea. God grant it may be at least the means of bringing you financial comfort. The other five letters I have given to Thomas Beverly, J. Fell, J. S. Webster, J. Fitzgerald, and W. Wells. In these letters I gave a list of all my property, and will now give the same here. I have banked – there is such confusion I can hardly think – and now –

My God! What do I hear? The captain orders all into the ladies' cabin, as the water is pouring in again at the other end of the boat. No list of my property can be made now. The lights are going out. The worst is at hand.

This I can say: I had money and real estate. The boat rolls so I can't write much more.

I hereby write my last will and testament, giving you, Minnie Bowdish, everything belonging to me. This is done with death in sight. This is from your loving mother,

Jennie Parsons.

The story was reported all over the country and still appears in books of remarkable tales and shipwrecks: "The Bottled Will." Minnie claimed that since the lists of assets did not survive, she did not know where to look for them. She hired investigators, but they never found either real estate or bank accounts. Then, a quarter century later, she saw the advertisement looking for heirs, found the will pressed into a book, and came to San Francisco to claim her due.

There was a hearing in San Francisco, and the evidence was evaluated. Neil Henley was called back from Victoria to testify. One issue raised was that the letter clearly stated it was written at 6 PM, and Henley said that the collision did not occur much before 10 PM. Of the five men Jennie named as passengers on the *Pacific*, only Thomas Beverley is known to have been aboard, although many passengers were never recorded. But the States proved conclusively that Jennie Parsons arrived in the city of New York with her parents and sisters by the ship *Jennie Lind* on the 25th of February, 1852, five years after Jennie's supposed first marriage in New York. Minnie was declared a fraud and sent packing.

But then some relatives of Otis Parsons made a claim, saying that Jennie died first when the lifeboat was swamped; therefore Captain Parsons had survived her and had by law inherited her estate. Neil Henley was again called to testify. He said that he had seen Mrs. Parsons in the lifeboat, sixty feet from the *Pacific*. At that time Captain Parsons was standing on the deck of the steamer when it suddenly broke in two and sank[14]. Therefore he had died first and Jennie

---

[14] This conflicts with the initial published statements of both Jelley and Henley. Henley said the falling smokestack caused a wave that dashed the boat against the steamer and swamped it, Jelley that the stack clipped the boat. Both said the boat capsized before the steam sank. There is a large variation in the various published testimony of the two men, and it is impossible to know which are accurate.

was still the owner of her estate when she died. The States were awarded the money.

The image of Jennie Mandeville in the boat, holding her dead son and watching her husband drown, is not a pleasant one.

David Higgins

In 1907, thirty-two years after the event, David Higgins, the man who saw so many of his friends off on their final voyage, wrote a memoir about the terrible effects of the loss of the *Pacific* on many families in both Victoria and San Francisco – widows and orphans thrown on the dole, spouses bereft, a lover driven mad, businesses ruined, at least two suicides, and whole families destroyed. He concluded:

> "I have often narrated the dreadful story of the loss of the *Pacific* to friends who had heard only a vague account of it, and on several occasions as I concluded the narrative, I have been asked which incident of the many pathetic ones connected with the wreck dwelt most in my mind. In other words, which of the occurrences that led up to the sinking impressed me most. I have always replied that, sweeping aside every consideration of sympathetic interest in the fate of many acquaintances who were rushed into eternity in an instant, as it were – forgetting for a time the awful sensations those on board the ship must have experienced when the truth was forced upon them that they were beyond human help and that the sun had set forever upon their earthly careers – I say I have always replied that the one picture which presents itself to my mind when I recall the awful event is that of the bonnie little blue-eyed boy to whom I said farewell as the gang plank was drawn in. I had never seen him before – he was neither

kith nor kin of mine – but whenever I think of the going down of the *Pacific* his sweet face appears to me – sometimes as I last saw it; and again wearing an expression of keen anguish and horror, the bright eyes filled with tears and the hands held out in a vain position to be saved from an impending doom. Since I sat down to write this sad story he has been with me every moment of the time; and once I thought I heard him repeat what I have often in the silent hours of the day or night imagined I heard him say: 'You placed me in this coffin; cannot you help me out?'

"Alas! If I had but known."

Made in the USA
Columbia, SC
07 December 2021